We Go!

Buses

Dana Meachen Rau

Marshall Cavendish
Benchmark
New York

We go on a bus.

3

Buses have wheels.

Buses have doors.

Buses have steps.

Buses have drivers.

11

Buses go on trips.

Buses go to camp.

15

Buses go to school.

We go on a bus!

Words to Know

camp bus

doors

driver

school bus

steps

tour bus

wheels

Index

Page numbers in **boldface** are illustrations.

About the Author

Dana Meachen Rau is the author of many other titles in the Bookworms series, as well as other nonfiction and early reader books. She lives in Burlington, Connecticut, with her husband and two children.

With thanks to the Reading Consultants:

Nanci Vargus, Ed.D., is an Assistant Professor of Elementary Education at the University of Indianapolis.

Beth Walker Gambro is an Adjunct Professor at the University of Saint Francis in Joliet, Illinois.

Marshall Cavendish Benchmark
99 White Plains Road
Tarrytown, New York 10591-9001
www.marshallcavendish.us

Text copyright © 2010 by Marshall Cavendish Corporation

Library of Congress Cataloging-in-Publication Data

Rau, Dana Meachen, 1971-
Buses / by Dana Meachen Rau.
p. cm. — (Bookworms. We go!)
Includes index.
Summary: "Describes the physical attributes, different kinds, and purposes of buses"—Provided by publisher.
ISBN 978-0-7614-4077-2
1. Buses—Juvenile literature. I. Title.
TL232.R352 2010
629.28'333—dc22
2008042501

Editor: Christina Gardeski
Publisher: Michelle Bisson
Designer: Virginia Pope
Art Director: Anahid Hamparian

Photo Research by Anne Burns Images

Cover Photo by *Corbis*/Najlah Feanny

The photographs in this book are used with permission and through the courtesy of:
Alamy Images: pp. 1, 17, 20BR David R. Frazier; pp. 11, 20BL eStock Photo. *Corbis*: p. 3 Gabe Palmer;
pp. 13, 21TR Fridmar Damm/zefa. *SuperStock*: pp. 5, 15, 20TL, 21B age fotostock; pp. 7, 20TR Mauritius;
pp. 9, 21TL James J. Bissell. *Terry Wilder Stock*: p. 19.

Printed in Malaysia
1 3 5 6 4 2